RIHANNA
Bad Girl

Publisher and Creative Director: Nick Wells
Project Editors: Polly Prior and Catherine Taylor
Picture Research: Laura Bulbeck
Art Director and Layout Design: Mike Spender
Digital Design and Production: Chris Herbert

Special thanks to: Stephen Feather, Dawn Laker and Daniela Nava

FLAME TREE PUBLISHING

Crabtree Hall, Crabtree Lane
Fulham, London SW6 6TY
United Kingdom

www.flametreepublishing.com

First published 2012

12 14 16 15 13
1 3 5 7 9 10 8 6 4 2

Flame Tree Publishing is part of The Foundry Creative Media Co. Ltd

Chapters DEC 2 0 2012 $57.99

A CIP record for this book is available from the British Library upon request.

ISBN 978-0-85775-275-8

Printed in China

RIHANNA
Bad Girl

MICHAEL HEATLEY AND GRAHAM BETTS

FOREWORD: MANGO SAUL, EDITOR OF SUGARSCAPE.COM

FLAME TREE
PUBLISHING

Contents

Foreword

Welcome Rihanna fan. Yes, you.

You're the Barbadian singer's number one obsessive; why else did you pick up this book? From her humble beginnings looking for a record label to being known around the world, this book has everything you need. It could easily just be a list, spitting out facts and records that Rihanna's broken over the last six years, but that would be very dull.

I had the pleasure of interviewing Robyn Rihanna Fenty in 2005, just after her debut 'Pon De Replay' hit Number 2 in the singles charts. She was a shy 17 year old, who had been catapulted to fame with her infectious first single. From the moment she walked into the room I knew she was going to be a global megastar. What surprised me that day was not only was she beautiful, she knew exactly how to answer a journalist's questions – her attention to detail was immaculate, despite her teenage years. Since then, some five years and over 20 million sold albums later, the girl from Saint Michael hasn't stopped. And, it doesn't stop with music: Rihanna tirelessly works for numerous charities and is now about to star in a film – there seems to be no boundaries to her talent...

Rihanna's knack of producing amazing music is truly a gift from above. So here it is, her life and music so far, in candid pictures and lots of thought. A perfect way to spend an evening...

Mango Saul, Editor, www.sugarscape.com

'It was perfect, really. We really took it for granted, but we basically spent the entire day on the beach with summer all year round. It wasn't special to us because that was just normal for Barbados.'

Rihanna

Barbados Beginnings

Up until 2005 the Caribbean island of Barbados had hardly set the musical world alight. Perhaps their most famous musical export was Bruce Brewster who, under the recording name Rayvon, had linked with Shaggy on the hits 'In The Summertime' and 'Angel' – the latter a 2001 UK chart topper. In spite of this lack of success, many dreamed of being the one who would buck the trend and become nationally and internationally successful. One of these dreamers was Rihanna, who was born Robyn Rihanna Fenty in Saint Michael on 20 February 1988. Her mother, Monica Braithwaite, was a retired accountant, while her father, Ronald Fenty, was a warehouse supervisor for a garment factory. Robyn, as she is still known to her family, is the oldest of three children, with brothers Rorrey and Rajad completing the family unit. Ronald also had three children from an earlier relationship, giving Robyn two half-sisters and a half-brother.

Singing To Escape

The family later moved to Bridgetown, where Robyn attended primary school at the Charles F. Broome Memorial School and then the Combermere School. Away from school, Robyn contributed to the household income by helping her father sell clothes on a street stall. She grew up listening to reggae music and began to sing at the age of seven. This was probably her way of shutting family problems out of her mind,

> *'I didn't get along with people very well. I got along with guys, but I hated the girls and the teachers. All my friends, even if they weren't in school, were always guys.'*
>
> *Rihanna*

as Robyn had to watch her parents' relationship going from bad to worse. Ronald's drug and alcohol addictions fuelled arguments and, sometimes, violence. By the time she was eight, she had begun to suffer severe headaches that convinced doctors she might be suffering from a brain tumour. When scans revealed nothing, stress was assumed to be the likely cause. Singing became an escape route, with the weather another consolation.

No Model Student

Robyn's father left the family when she was 14 and she was able to enjoy a less stressful home life. She and two of her schoolmates formed a musical trio, while Robyn also enrolled as an army cadet in a sub-military programme, where the future singer Shontelle was her drill sergeant. Robyn also harboured thoughts of graduating from high school, although she was, by her own admission, not the best of students. While there were aspects of school she enjoyed, there were others that were not so pleasant. Besides, Robyn had already decided she wished to pursue a career in music and for much of the time schoolwork was simply getting in the way. School was something to be tolerated, not enjoyed, and her musical trio provided something to look forward to in the evenings. Fortunately, a very good friend was about to make an introduction that would change her life.

'If I wasn't an **entertainer,** *I would still be in* **boring** *school studying* **psychology.** *I hate school so* **thank God** *I'm* **doing** *what I'm doing.'*

Rihanna

A Successful Audition

Among the regular holiday visitors to Barbados were renowned record producers Evan Rogers and Carl Sturken. Both were married to Barbadian women and so were often to be found on the island. It was during one such visit that Robyn's friend suggested to the producers that they should take a listen to Robyn and her trio. An audition was arranged at the hotel where Evan Rogers and his wife were staying. Rogers would later claim he knew Robyn would be a superstar the minute she walked into his hotel room, completely overshadowing her two bandmates. The trio performed their own version of Destiny's Child's 'Emotion', itself a cover of a song written by the Bee Gees. Suitably impressed, Rogers invited Robyn back for a second audition, asking her to come along with her mother but without her friends. This was now a solo star in waiting…

Back And Forth

It was at the second audition that Evan Rogers laid out a rough plan for the immediate future. Rogers and Sturken had some material they thought might be ideal for Robyn, which she was asked to record as demos in their studio. This meant Robyn and her mother shuttling back and forth between Barbados and Stamford in Connecticut, as the sessions had to be scheduled during the various school holidays. Although Robyn could see a future career on the horizon, she was not allowed to turn her back on school altogether. There were to be some welcome distractions during this time, with Robyn winning the Miss Combermere school beauty pageant and her high school talent show, for which she performed Mariah Carey's 'Hero'. With her combination of musical talent and good looks, this pupil was on the way to top showbiz grades!

'My mom said, "You are not stopping school until you get signed." And even when I got signed, she still made me go to school.'

Rihanna

The Demo Goes Out

By January 2005 the first four-track demo recording was complete and ready to be sent out. Among the songs it contained was a cover of 'For The Love Of You' and two new compositions: the ballad 'Last Time' and the quirky 'Pon De Replay'. Meanwhile, Rogers and Sturken had carefully selected the record companies they were to target with Robyn's demo, including most of the major players in urban music. Several responded almost immediately, and by February 2005 Robyn had an itinerary before her that would decide her future career. One of the meetings was with Def Jam, where A&R executive Jay Brown had passed the demo on to Jay-Z, the label president at the time, and LA Reid, the head of Island Def Jam Recordings.

Signing With Def Jam

With maturity beyond her tender years, Robyn sang 'For The Love Of You' to two of the most important men in the American record industry. Jay-Z was convinced that 'Pon De Replay' was strong enough to become a major hit, but he was concerned that Robyn would become a one-hit wonder. 'When a song is that big, it's hard to come back from. I don't sign songs; I sign artists.' Fortunately for Robyn, her audition proved she had the star quality required to develop a whole career, with 'Pon De Replay' simply providing the launch pad. Jay-Z and LA Reid took little time in reaching a decision: they wanted Robyn signed to their label and they wanted it done

'Def Jam was the *first* label to call back. We got *other* calls, but they were the most **enthusiastic**. It was so nerve-wracking, though, the *whole* experience.' *Rihanna*

immediately. Robyn and her team were not allowed out of the building until the contract was signed and sealed; all the meetings scheduled with other labels were cancelled. Robyn was officially a Def Jam artist.

Becoming Rihanna

Of course, signing the contract was just the first step in Robyn's career. The singer chose to work under her middle name, Rihanna, since there was already another female by the name of Robyn (a Swedish singer who enjoyed a big hit in 1998 with 'Show Me Love'). No sooner was the ink dry on the contract than the decision was made to relocate to New York, living with Evan Rogers and his wife, and working around the clock for the next three months in order to complete what would become her debut album: *Music Of The Sun*. There were also opportunities to work with other artists, with Rihanna guesting on Memphis Bleek's fourth studio album, *534*. However, this was a minor diversion from the job in hand: creating the Rihanna persona both on and off record.

'In the *beginning*, it was really *strict* for me. We had a *young* fan base, and they were trying to keep *me fresh*. I wanted to be *sassy*, the *attitude*, all these things that *I am*.'

Rihanna

'When I first heard 'Pon De Replay', I didn't want to do it because it was very sing-songy and very ... whatever. But after I started recording it, I went along with it and started liking it.'

Rihanna

The First Album

Until the time she became firmly established as a star, Rihanna had to accept that she needed to be moulded by those who knew better. In the studio, this meant recording whatever might be put in front of her. With 'Pon De Replay' an obvious starting point, it was decided that the debut album should be largely reggae-influenced, as Rihanna would be marketed within reggae circles because of her Caribbean heritage, even though it was Jamaica, rather than Barbados, that was more readily associated with the music.

'Pon De Replay'

Rihanna had first heard 'Pon De Replay' during her early discussions with producer Evan Rogers and was not particularly impressed. But Rogers convinced her it would be a hit and, more importantly, it was a song both Jay-Z and Def Jam felt would be the ideal career launcher. As Jay-Z and LA Reid had predicted, 'Pon De Replay' became a huge international hit. In the US, Rihanna's new homeland, the single raced up the *Billboard* charts, peaking at No. 2; 'Pon De Replay' matched that success in the UK. As disappointing as missing out on the top spot might have been, there was little time to get despondent, for her debut album was also hitting the shops as August came to an end and the public's response to it would be what determined whether Rihanna was to be the next big thing or last week's news.

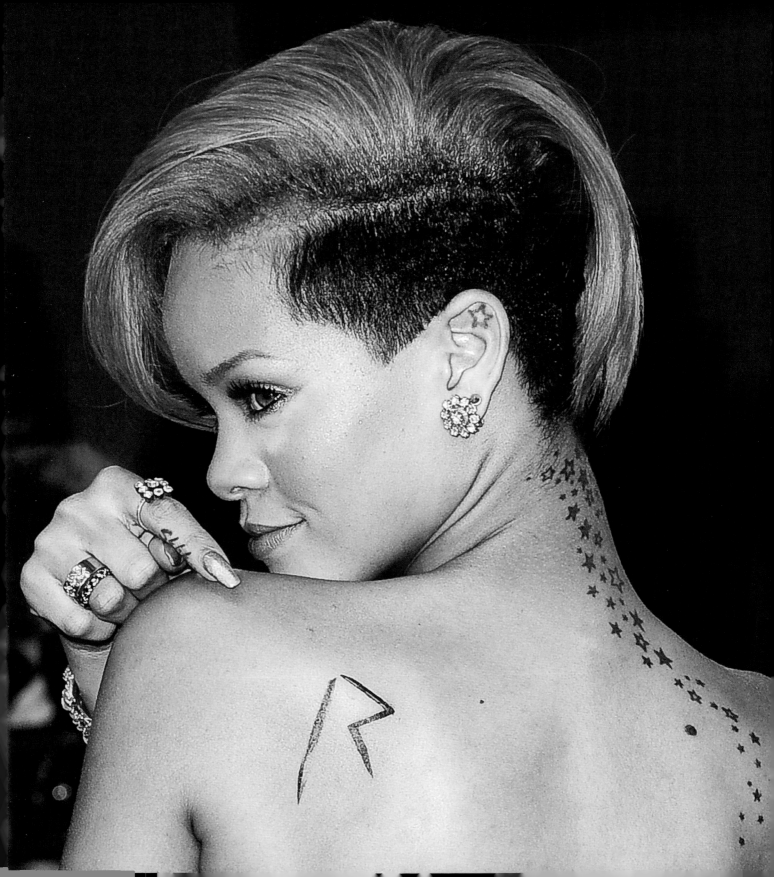

> *'I would have **never** dreamed that **my career** would be this successful. I grew up in an average home in Barbados, and we didn't live in the best neighborhood.'*
>
> *Rihanna*

Music Of The Sun

Music Of The Sun was an album that flitted from one musical style to another, taking in dancehall, R&B and hip-hop, trying one minute to establish Rihanna as the new dancehall diva on tracks such as 'Pon De Replay' and 'You Don't Love Me', and the next going down the same musical path as Beyoncé on the heavy R&B numbers 'Let Me' and 'Rush'. Collaborations with J-Status, Vybz Kartel, Kardinall Offishall and Elephant Man ensured interest from the hip-hop market, while Rihanna's contribution was that of a more than competent vocalist. Fortunately, numbers such as 'Now I Know' and 'Last Time' pointed to a brighter future and allowed Rihanna to prove that there was an exceptional voice to go with all of the studio trickery. *Music Of The Sun* sold in excess of 500,000 copies in the US, peaking at No. 10 on the *Billboard* Top 200 and earning Rihanna a gold disc. In the UK the album barely made the Top 40, spending a solitary week at No. 35.

A Girl Like Rihanna

Work on *A Girl Like Me* commenced in September 2005, barely a month after the release of its predecessor. This time around the collaborations came from J-Status, Dwane Husbands and Sean Paul, and the material covered much the same dancehall and hip-hop territory as *Music Of The Sun*. One big difference was the fact that Rihanna was able to input her own thoughts and ideas into the album's

Ne-Yo is one of the sweetest, sweetest people I've ever met, ever worked with. He's an amazing songwriter. So we finally got to meet and he's like, "Yeah, we gotta do something."

Rihanna

creation, discussing with Reid the notion of incorporating a rock feel into the final mix. It was also Rihanna's idea to work with Ne-Yo, a songwriter she much admired for his work with the likes of Mario. Indeed, Ne-Yo and Rihanna had discussed collaboration while recording *Music Of The Sun*, but the timing at that moment was not right.

Variations On A Theme

While *Music Of The Sun* was recorded over three months, virtually on a daily basis, the follow-up album was recorded here and there, fitting in recording sessions around promotional work for the debut album. It made for some crazy hours as Rihanna had to perform live shows and then fly in to lay down her vocals on one track after another. Although the recording sessions were disjointed, there was a theme holding the album together, with Rihanna keen to express what it was like to be 'a girl like me'. She came up with the album's title and was also able to use her own experiences, including touring as the opening act for Gwen Stefani, to help craft three of the songs on it. Little wonder the album had more of a Rihanna feel than its predecessor.

SOS Success

The album's lead single was to be 'SOS', written by Evan Bogart and Jonathan Rotem. Although Rihanna was unfamiliar with Soft Cell's 'Tainted Love', which provides the song with the bass line and tempo, it was clear that the combination of the new and old was a winning formula, with 'SOS' likely to get considerable club action.

Three videos were made of the song, including promos in support of Agent Provocateur and Nike. Commercial

[A Girl Like Me is] a very personal album; it's my baby. It's all about what it's like to be a girl like me ...'

Rihanna

considerations were an important area of music promotion, and Rihanna's instant rapport with the youth of the day made her an ideal 'spokeswoman' for a wide variety of brands.

Top Of The Pops

Released as a single on 7 March 2006, 'SOS' received instant airplay acceptance, also aided by its inclusion in the film soundtrack to *Bring It On: All Or Nothing* in which Rihanna also had a cameo role. The result was a sure-fire smash, flying up the *Billboard* chart and knocking Daniel Powter's 'Bad Day' off the summit. 'SOS' became Rihanna's first American chart topper and spent three weeks at No. 1, further fuelling demand for her second album. The single also did well internationally, hitting No. 2 in the UK, where it was unable to dislodge Gnarls Barkley's 'Crazy', and topping the charts in several key markets. The promotion for *A Girl Like Me* got off to the strongest possible start, with Rihanna well on her way to capturing charts and hearts across the globe.

Second Time Around

A Girl Like Me was released barely eight months after Rihanna's debut album had hit the streets and it shifted 115,000 copies in its first week – nearly twice the opening sales of the debut. The success of the first album and its

'We were so *busy* promoting the *first album* while trying to get this one done, working some *crazy* hours. That's why this *album* is so close to me, 'cause I really put my *heart* and *soul* into it.

Rihanna

'We just felt it was time. It made no sense waiting ... That's what's great about the music business. When you feel it's time, you just go for it.'

Rihanna

singles, including 'SOS', ensured instant interest, and *A Girl Like Me* appeared on the *Billboard* chart at No. 5; it would go on to sell over 1.3 million copies, earning Rihanna a platinum disc from the RIAA. In the UK the album debuted at No.6 in April 2006, although it was later to surpass this opening mark as it enjoyed a revival of interest following the release of the second single. The album sold nearly 600,000 copies in the UK, easily earning Rihanna a platinum award. Indeed, the sales success enjoyed by *A Girl Like Me* (it would be the twentieth bestselling album in the world for 2006) served to prove that an album does not have to be critically acclaimed to be widely accepted.

Steady Seller

It was the personal touch that made the album so popular with Rihanna's record-buying public. While the critics may have been in two minds, the public had no problems accepting Rihanna and the music she was producing, rapidly turning her into a major player on the charts around the world. The second single, 'Unfaithful', became a Top 10 success in multiple territories, including the US (it peaked at No. 6) and the UK, where it entered the chart at No. 16. It was then involved in a week-long battle with McFly for the top spot, missing out by a handful of sales and having to settle for a No. 2 peak. Compensation of sorts was achieved by the parent album rebounding up the charts to hit a new peak of No. 5 on the back of the continued success of this single.

Riding To Reward

'We Ride' was chosen as the third single from the album in many territories, although it met with a mixed reception. The US even went so far as to cull a fourth single from the album, releasing 'Break It Off' in December 2006. Featuring a guest appearance from Sean Paul, 'Break It Off' returned Rihanna to the Top 10, peaking at No. 9. This chart placing was made all the more remarkable by the fact that the single did not have an accompanying video. In 2006 Rihanna collected awards for Best R&B Act from both the MOBOs and MTV Europe Music Awards, indicating that, as far as Europe was concerned, she

'The best advice I had is: "Keep good people around you, because if you have a **strong circle** then it's *hard for negativity* to get in."'

Rihanna

*'We've been **prepping** for the tour for a **few** months now, **coming out** with **different ideas** and **cool things** that we can do.'*

Rihanna

had made the transition to superstar status. Added to these prestigious awards were nominations for Best New Artist and Viewers' Choice from the MTV Video Music Awards. Rihanna was set to become a regular at award shows and ceremonies in the years to come.

Headlining Tour

By mid-2006 Rihanna was considered ready to headline her own tour. Starting in San Francisco, the tour would take in the United States and Canada in North America and Jamaica during the course of some 36 dates between 1 July and 29 September. Featuring the likes of Ciara, Trey Songz and J-Status as openers (a total of seven different acts were selected), the tour also took in various festivals, including the Reggae Sumfest. Having made the first tentative steps as a headliner, Rihanna was then part of the Rock Tha Block Tour and linked up with The Pussycat Dolls for their PCD Tour of the United Kingdom and later with The Black Eyed Peas. These two tours in particular exposed Rihanna to a whole new audience.

A Change In Direction

Rihanna may have made her initial breakthrough with the distinct reggae flavour of 'Pon De Replay' and the general feel to her second album, but she knew better than anyone that she would have to evolve her music and her style to

'That album I listen to all day, all night. When I was in the studio that was the album that I listened to all the time and I really admired that every song was a great song. You could listen to the entire album. And I was like, "I have to make an album like this."'

Rihanna on Afrodisiac

stay at the top of the charts. The safe ground covered by her first two albums would have to be abandoned for the third. Besides, while reggae and dancehall might be popular for a track or two, they did not have the kind of appeal that would endure over a whole album. Rihanna was certain she would need to leave reggae and dancehall behind. Instead, alongside the rock music she had been listening to since coming to America, she looked towards a much more urban style, focusing on the music some of her peers were turning out and in particular on Brandy's *Afrodisiac*.

The New Team

Prior to the recording sessions for *Good Girl Gone Bad*, Rihanna sat down with executives from Def Jam to map out a strategy. The resulting album would draw upon a bigger pool of writers and producers, including Ne-Yo, Stargate, Timbaland and Christopher Stewart, as well as the tried and tested Evan Rogers and Carl Sturken. This combination crafted a series of both uptempo and ballad material, covering pop and dance-pop, as Rihanna targeted an even wider audience. Indeed, the basic concept for the album was that it should appeal to someone, somewhere, so that even if a single failed in one market, it would find a niche in another. Rihanna also used the success of the singles from her previous album as a template for the new album, with danceable rhythms underscoring the majority of the tracks. Press and public alike awaited the results with interest.

The Downpour Starts

'Umbrella' became the lead single and the track that heralded the arrival of an international superstar. Written by Christopher Stewart, Terius Nash and Thaddis Harrell, the song had been offered to Britney Spears but was turned down by her record company because they believed she already had enough material. It was then considered for Mary J. Blige and Taio

> "When the demo [of 'Umbrella'] first started playing, I was like, "This is interesting; this is weird ..." I listened to it over and over. I said, "I need this record. I want to record it tomorrow.""
>
> *Rihanna*

Cruz (apparently, he loved the song but was unable to convince his label of its worth), but fortunately LA Reid stepped in and pinpointed the track as ideal for Rihanna. Even with approval so far up the executive ladder, it was not a given that Rihanna would record the song, since Christopher Stewart expressed his reluctance as to whether she was the right artist for the track. Fortunately, once the team worked in the studio and Rihanna laid down the now infamous 'Ella ella' catchphrase, everyone present realized they were on to something special.

Hands-on Rihanna

The recordings for *Good Girl Gone Bad* took place between October 2006 and the following April at the Westlake Recording Studios in Los Angeles. Among the contributors on the vocals were Jay-Z, Ne-Yo, Justin Timberlake and Timbaland – all artists Rihanna had expressed admiration for and who would enable her to adopt a more pop-orientated persona. For this album, Rihanna took a much more hands-on approach when it came to selecting material, even going so far as to question the sense of the lyrics from the various writers if their meanings were not entirely obvious during the first readthrough – she wanted not only to sing songs in which she believed, but to understand every one of them too. It was at this time, in the studio, that Rihanna finally took control of her own destiny.

'I want to keep people dancing but still be soulful at the same time. You feel different every album and at this stage I feel like I want to do a lot of uptempo songs.'

Rihanna

Top Of The World

The release of *Good Girl Gone Bad* would still have been eagerly anticipated because of the success of her earlier recordings, but the international success of 'Umbrella' catapulted it into a different arena altogether. Heavy airplay ahead of release ensured that 'Umbrella' was the most talked-about single in many a year, racking up thousands of pre-order sales. It was eventually released in the US in March 2007 and was soon relentlessly climbing the chart; during the course of one week in June, it jumped from No. 42 to No. 1, where it would remain for seven weeks without a break. It would go on to repeat that success in 27 other countries around the world and earn positive reviews from virtually all sections of the media. The combination of Rihanna and rapper Jay-Z had been nothing less than a masterstroke.

'This album didn't feel rushed; it came effortlessly and it felt like the perfect time. I love summertime and I always bring a single out for the summer.'

Rihanna

Let It Rain

The single's performance in the UK was almost without precedent. In its first week it sold over 34,000 downloads, and Rihanna became the first female artist to enter the UK charts at pole position on downloads only. 'Umbrella' remained at No. 1 the following week too, still on download sales alone. The following week, with the release of a physical edition, the track remained at the top of the chart and went on to spend 10 consecutive weeks at No.1. American sales of *Good Girl Gone Bad* topped 162,000 units in its first week, while in the UK – where the album debuted at No. 1 – it proved to be the bestselling album of Rihanna's career, going five-times platinum (sales in excess of 1.5 million) and remaining on the charts for more than four years.

'Shut Up And Drive'

In the same way that Michael Jackson's *Thriller* and *Bad* albums had churned out hit single after hit single, so *Good Girl Gone Bad* set about turning itself into a one-album greatest hits package. No fewer than eight singles would eventually see the light of day and the vast majority found their way into the Top 20. The second single to be lifted was 'Shut Up And Drive', a more rock-orientated single than any of her previous releases. It would peak at No. 15 on the *Billboard* Hot 100, as the American audience found it too radical a departure from her earlier efforts. It performed significantly

'Am I sick of singing "Umbrella"? No, I don't think I'll ever tire of it because it means so much to me. Every time I hear the first bars it feels brand new.'

Rihanna

better in the UK, hitting No. 5 while 'Umbrella' was still in the Top 20 and slowly winding its way down the chart.

'Hate That I Love You'

As if to prove the sometimes subtle differences between what makes a successful single in the US compared with the UK, 'Hate That I Love You', which featured Ne-Yo, reversed its chart performances on either side of the Atlantic. In the US it returned Rihanna to the Top 10, peaking at No. 7 and making the Top 20 in over 15 countries. That tally did include the UK, where it had to settle for a rather more modest final position of No. 15, even though Rihanna performed the song on the Royal Variety Show. Meanwhile, 'Umbrella' was still setting records and collecting awards, earning Rihanna two MTV Video Music Awards for Video of the Year and Monster Single of the Year in September 2007 – and this was not to be the end of the accolades this particular song would collect.

'When it *first starts off,* you think it's a *sexy song,* but you have to *listen* to the *lyrics.* It's a really *deep song.'*

Rihanna on 'Hate That I Love You'

World Domination

In September 2007 Rihanna started her *Good Girl Gone Bad* world tour, performing some 80 concerts across five continents over the course of 15 months. This hectic schedule also had to allow time to appear at various presentations, including the American Music Awards in Los Angeles in November 2007. Despite being up against Beyoncé and Fantasia in the Favourite Female Artist of the Soul/R&B Category, Rihanna collected the award on the night. The Grammy Awards, held at the turn of the year, honoured her with no fewer than four nominations: Best Rap/Sung Collaboration and Record of the Year (both for 'Umbrella'), Best Dance Recording (for 'Don't Stop The Music') and Best R&B Vocal Performance by a Duo (for 'Hate That I Love You', with Ne-Yo). In addition, 'Umbrella' picked up a nomination for Song of the Year and R&B Song of the Year for its writers.

'It's a very edgy album. Every song has a different element of a different genre. We got rock influences, we got Caribbean influences, some pop in there, as well as a 1980s vibe in it.'

Rihanna

Don't Stop The Hits

Based around a sample of Michael Jackson's 'Wanna Be Startin' Somethin'', 'Don't Stop The Music' was the next track chosen as a single from the album. Much more dance-orientated than previous releases, the track had already proved its worth by earning a Grammy nomination and topping the *Billboard* Hot Dance Club Play listings ahead of release. It bounced its way into the Top 10 around the globe, coming to rest at No. 3 in the US on the back of an astonishing 3 million-plus downloads. In several territories it became her most successful single to date, topping the charts in Austria, Belgium, France, Germany, Luxembourg, The Netherlands and Switzerland. In the UK it would reach No. 4, earn another gold disc and spend 31 weeks on the chart. Certainly you could not visit a club or turn on the radio without hearing it.

'We figured Good Girl Gone Bad was the perfect title because it showed people I'm my own person now. I'm not the innocent Rihanna any more. I'm taking a lot more risks and chances.' Rihanna

Grammy Award

In addition to her four nominations for a Grammy, Rihanna had also been honoured with an invitation to perform at the ceremony in February 2008. She was up against stiff opposition in all four categories, including 'Rehab' by Amy Winehouse in both Record of the Year and Song of the Year. Noting that she had received nominations for more than one song, Rihanna chose to perform a medley of 'Umbrella' and 'Don't Stop The Music' for her performance. Later came the crowning moment; despite the fierce competition, it was announced that the Grammy Award for Best Rap/Sung Collaboration had been won by Rihanna featuring Jay-Z. While it was the fifth Grammy Award for Jay-Z, it was a first for Rihanna. And even though that was the only award she won that evening, it was not to be her last Grammy.

'Take A Bow'

Plans were already under way to reissue the *Good Girl Gone Bad* album with additional tracks and remixes. Ahead of this came a new single, 'Take A Bow', again written by Stargate (Tor Hermansen, Mikkel Eriksen and Shaffer Smith). If there was a magic ingredient for producing a hit record, then this team had apparently discovered it, for 'Take A Bow' became an instant smash the world over, hitting the Top 10 at the very least across the globe. It reserved its best performances for Canada, where it registered the biggest ever leap within the chart to No. 1; the US, where it would top the Hot Digital

My first single on my third album was perfect timing, and it was the perfect song to do with [Jay-Z]. Just being on the video set, it had me tripped out a little bit … it's crazy!'

Rihanna

*'It's not like we have a **rule** about putting out an **album** a year. Whatever I'm **feeling**, whatever I'm going through, whatever **mood** I'm in ... If I'm feeling like **dancing** or **clubbing**, then it will be **reflected** in the **music**.'*

Rihanna

Tracks, Hot Digital Songs, Hot R&B/Hip-Hop Songs (for the first time in her career), Hot R&B/Hip-Hop Airplay and Hot 100 charts; and the UK, where it was at the top for two weeks.

Reloaded

The success of 'Take A Bow' had whetted the appetite for the forthcoming release of *Good Girl Gone Bad: Reloaded*. In the UK, the original album had fallen as far as No. 66 on the album chart in May, but the sudden arrival of the remixed and extended version breathed new life into it, returning it to the Top 10 on 28 June and keeping it inside the Top 20 for the next five months. Further singles' success would have a constant effect on the album, which enjoyed a surge in sales as each new one was released. The US showed much the same result; the week the new edition became available, it leapt from No. 124 to No. 7 on the *Billboard* Top 200: a 930 per cent sales increase! Little wonder it ended the year as one of the bestselling albums.

Remix

'If I Never See Your Face Again' was originally written by Adam Levine and James Valentine of Maroon 5 and recorded for their 2007 album *It Won't Be Soon Before Long*. Somewhere along the way, Adam Levine constructed the song so that lyrically it was a battle of the sexes and looked for a suitable artist with whom to do a remix. Since Maroon 5 had attended several of Rihanna's shows and discovered there was a mutual admiration, it made sense to approach her to see if she wanted to do a collaboration. Rihanna later announced she was honoured to be involved, while Adam would state, 'It sounds cheesy, but if the magic is there, if the chemistry is there, you don't even have to think about it.' The new version of 'If I Never See Your Face Again' was first performed live on MTV and received positive acclaim, leading to its eventual release as a single.

'I've always been a fan of Maroon 5. I love the energy of the song and the lyrics are badass, so I was psyched to do it.' Rihanna

'The video shoot was fun, but it was difficult to get serious for the seductive scenes because Adam and I are friends. We would bust out laughing on every other shot – that was the best part.'

Rihanna

Minor Blip

Rihanna has said that the video she made with Maroon 5 to support the single, directed by Anthony Mandler, was one of her favourites and that she enjoyed the whole experience of filming it. Despite the strong video, in which she and Adam flirt throughout, the single did not perform as well as might have been expected from the combination of two such hot acts. In the US the single peaked at No. 51 and in the UK it had to settle for a final position of No. 28 – the lowest charting of a Rihanna single up to that point. Despite the relative failure of the single, the public still continued to purchase the *Reloaded* album in droves, resulting in yet another appearance in the UK Top 10. It was time to unleash yet another monster in 'Disturbia'.

Back To Winning Ways

Almost as soon as it became clear that 'If I Never See Your Face Again' was not going to be a monster single, plans were made for the release of one of the other new tracks on *Reloaded*. 'Disturbia' was written by Rihanna's then-boyfriend and fellow singer Chris Brown, along with Brian Kennedy Seals, Andre Merritt and Robert Allen. It was originally intended for Chris himself, but on reflection the team decided that it suited a female singer better and so offered it to Rihanna. She took to the song immediately, even going so far as to present it personally to LA Reid in order to convince him that not only did she want to record it, but she also

> *'It was the first time Rihanna actually came to me and said, "Here's the song I want to put out." That was her taking control. She's at that place where she can do that.'*
>
> *LA Reid*

wanted it issued as a single. Reid duly agreed, noting that Rihanna was showing a good grasp of what made a hit record.

'Disturbia'

Initially released on 17 June as a digital single in the US, 'Disturbia' would generate more than 3 million downloads in that territory (it has since topped the 4 million mark) and would go on to replace Katy Perry's 'I Kissed A Girl' at the top of the singles chart. In the UK, digital and physical sales were enough to propel the single to No. 3 (behind Eric Prydz' 'Pjanoo' and Perry) and enable it to hover around the charts for over nine months – the third single by Rihanna to achieve such a feat. 'Disturbia' also collected further sales awards for the singer to place on what had to be by then an overloaded sideboard, for it was to attain gold status in the UK. It also went on to earn similar achievements on a worldwide basis as it hit the Top 10 in 15 European countries and topped the New Zealand charts.

'Rehab'

The sales impact of Rihanna and her *Good Girl Gone Bad: Reloaded* album continued to show little sign of diminishing, prompting the release of an eighth single from the album: 'Rehab', featuring Justin Timberlake. At much the same time, Rihanna could also be heard guesting on T.I.'s single 'Live Your Life', giving her a two-pronged attack on the world's charts. 'Live Your Life' turned out to be the better performer, topping the US charts for six weeks, while 'Rehab' had to settle for a final position of No. 18. In the UK it was much the same story: 'Live Your Life' hit No. 2 while 'Rehab' made a more modest No. 18. However, once again the *Reloaded* album enjoyed the additional attention, moving up to No. 2 on the UK album chart – tantalizingly close to reclaiming the top spot but unable to dislodge Kings of Leon.

'[Justin] wrote the song in his head. He didn't write anything on paper. He went into the booth and sang it and I was very, very impressed. We all loved it.' Rihanna

The Final Tally

If ever there were an album that vindicated an artist's decision to take greater control on their career and destiny, then that album was undoubtedly *Good Girl Gone Bad*. The original version sold a combined total of more than 2.6 million copies in the US alone. In the UK, sales were not that far behind, having shifted 1.7 million copies. Total sales around the globe topped the 5.8 million mark, making it the third bestselling album worldwide released in 2007 (only the soundtrack to *High School Musical* and Linkin Park's *Minutes To Midnight* managed to better it). Not surprisingly, Def Jam moved swiftly to secure a longer-term contract for the artist described as 'Diva of the Year' for 2008.

Beating Mariah

As 2008 came to a close, there were more awards and nominations to reflect Rihanna's success. November 2008 saw the singer storm the American Music Awards with victory in the Favourite Soul/R&B Female Artist category, thus becoming the first female artist to win conseculive awards in this category since Natalie Cole and Aretha Franklin achieved this feat during the 1970s. However, it was indicative of the inroads Rihanna had made on pop music – and not just R&B/Soul – that she should also be nominated for the Favourite Pop/Rock Female Artist category. Having performed 'Rehab' at the show, broadcast live from the Nokia Theater in Los Angeles on 23 November, it was announced that the

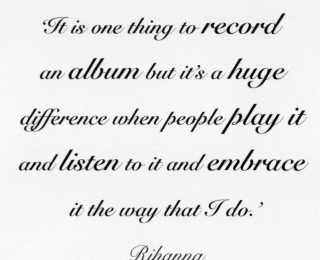

'It is one thing to *record* an *album* but it's a *huge* difference when people *play* it and *listen* to it and *embrace* it the way that I do.'

Rihanna

winner in this category was neither Mariah Carey, nor Alicia Keys (who had also been up against Rihanna in the R&B/Soul category); it was Rihanna.

More Nominations

Having topped most of the annual magazine polls (most notably, *Billboard*'s Year-End Charts as the Top Pop Artist – Female for both singles and albums; Top Hot 100 Singles Artist – Female; Top Pop 100 Artist; Top Digital Songs Artist; Top Hot Mainstream Top 40 Artist and Top Hot Dance Airplay Artist), Rihanna could also look forward to the forthcoming Grammy Awards show at which she was scheduled to perform. The nominations had seen her pick up entries in three categories: Best Pop Collaboration with Vocals for 'If I Never See Your Face Again' with Maroon 5; Best Dance Recording for 'Disturbia'; and Best Music Video, Long Form for *Good Girl Gone Bad Live*. Once again, it was the diversity of the nominations that showed Rihanna was broadening her appeal beyond her initial R&B fanbase and into all areas of the music market.

'To me, that song ["Rehab"] is the bridge for her to be accepted as an adult in the music industry.'

Justin Timberlake

Battles Of A Different Kind

'The more *in love* we became, the more **dangerous** we became for each other, *equally* ... dangerous. He was my **best friend**, the person I loved. We spent **two years** of our lives **together**.' *Rihanna*

As the great and the good of the music industry gathered at the Staples Center in Los Angeles on 8 February 2009 for the Grammys, there was one noticeable absentee: Rihanna. Her aides announced that she was cancelling her scheduled appearance and chose at the time not to elaborate further as to why she would not be appearing. With much of the post-ceremony publicity focusing on the success of Alison Krauss and Robert Plant, who jointly won five awards, there was some speculation as to why Rihanna had pulled out. Some reasoned that it was because she won nothing and therefore had nothing

to collect on the night, although Rihanna would not have known she was going to end the evening empty-handed. Then, nearly a month after the event, reports surfaced that her boyfriend Chris Brown had been charged with assault and making criminal threats.

The Full Story

Gradually, a more complete and detailed story emerged of the events that led to Rihanna cancelling not only her appearance at the Grammy Awards, but also the NAACP Image Awards and the Asian leg of her touring schedule. Rihanna had been the victim of an assault by Brown on the day of the show and had been left visibly battered and bruised, and certainly in no state to perform or appear in public at the time. Eventually, Brown would be handed a sentence of five years on probation, one year of domestic violence counselling and six months of community service. There was also a five-year restraining order placed upon him, requiring him to remain 46 m (50 yards) away from Rihanna, or 9 m (10 yards) whenever the pair were at the same public event. The assault impacted quite considerably on Brown, with his music dropped from the playlists and a proposed UK tour cancelled when he was refused a visa.

Rihanna's Side

Although the original assault had been terrifying, it appeared initially as though Rihanna did not want to pursue the matter

'I don't have a desire at all to be with him. I don't see how we could get back together. But I'm not God, so I can't predict the future.'

Rihanna

further. Certainly it was not Rihanna who made a complaint to the police; it was Chris Brown turning himself in that alerted the media to the problem. Indeed, for a time it seemed as though the pair might be able to resume their relationship, which both admitted had been volatile. The restraining order effectively brought that to an end. Later, in November 2009, Rihanna appeared on the *20/20* programme with Diane Sawyer and spoke about the events of that evening, confirming that her relationship with Chris Brown was finally over for good.

Back To Music

Rihanna had little time to dwell on the incident with Chris Brown because, one month after the cancelled Grammy appearance, work was to begin on her fourth album, eventually titled *Rated R*. Once again, a wide pool of writers and producers were brought in to craft the album, with each having their own ideas as to how Rihanna should progress from her previous album. Ne-Yo felt that, while he could not write a song that was specifically about Rihanna and Chris Brown – partly as he was friendly with Brown – he could channel the anger that Rihanna must be feeling to both their advantages. He believed he could fashion an edgier and angrier album for her. Akon, meanwhile, wanted to produce material at the other end of the spectrum, lightening up her image. The battles between the teams certainly produced an interesting batch of songs for Rihanna to record…

'Even if Chris never hit me again, who is to say that their boyfriend won't? These are young girls, and I just didn't realize how much of an impact I had on these girls' lives until that happened. It was a wake-up call.'

Rihanna

Rated R

While Ne-Yo might have stated that he would not be writing a song about Rihanna's domestic battles, the media and critics would look intently at the contents of *Rated R* and try to establish a link between each respective song and the incident. What was 'Stupid In Love', 'Cold Case Love' or 'Rude Boy' if not about Rihanna's relationship with Chris Brown? Irrespective of the inspiration for the lyrics, the overall feel of the album was certainly harder than its predecessors. While this might have aided its performance in the US, it was to the detriment of the album in the international market. *Rated R* shifted 181,000 copies in its first week in the US, beating her previous best by some 13,000 copies. The album also hit No. 4 on the *Billboard* Top 200, becoming the fourth of her albums to make the Top 10 and second only to its immediate predecessor in terms of chart performance. *Rated R* would eventually earn a platinum award, although the final sales were less than half of those achieved by *Good Girl Gone Bad*.

'Run This Town'

While the material on *Rated R* was being completed, Rihanna found time to work with Jay-Z and Kanye West on the 'Run This Town' single. Featuring the three biggest names in the musical world at the time, it was, according to

Jay-Z, the prestige of the three artists that had been the inspiration for the song. 'We basically run this town. It's myself, Rihanna and Kanye West. It's pretty much it.' The result was never in doubt: an obvious smash that topped the charts in the UK for a single week and peaked at No. 2 in the US, where it became Jay-Z's biggest single success in around three years.

Twitter Debate

Rihanna has regularly used her Twitter account (@rihanna, established in October 2009) to keep in touch with her fans and is one of the few pop stars in complete control of her account. In return, she has gathered nearly 7.5 million followers. She is also one of the only pop stars talking back to their haters. Her Top 10 comebacks to abusive messages have made a feature on a celebrity website. But in May 2011 fans were shocked to find that not only was her ex-boyfriend Chris Brown following her on Twitter, but she was following him back. They were not happy to see their favourite singer showing any signs of reconciliation with her abusive ex, even if only on a social media site. One fan actually challenged her on following her violent ex-boyfriend, tweeting at her: 'I never thought you would go back to him! You better not, it's your life but you do have [people] that look up to you, e.g. young girls.'

I really like the boom [of Rated R], the grime of it. But if I were to combine that with more energetic, uptempo pop records, then I think that would be a happy marriage.'

Rihanna

'People go through their career dreaming of a collaboration with Jay-Z and here I am … it's very nerve-wracking but very exciting.' Rihanna

Ri Rules Facebook

If stardom is measured by how many Facebook fans you have, then Rihanna looks down on the competition from a lofty height. While Lady Gaga was first to ten million, Rihanna surpassed her in the summer of 2011 as both ladies soared through the 40 million barrier on the popular social networking site. It's believed Ri's account is updated by one or more ghostwriters, and the result lacks the personal touch of her Twitter account, but there's little doubt that she understands the value of updating her fans through the medium they know, love and use every day. She has sub-pages for videos and music, events (where fans can tell her they're going to her concerts) and a photo gallery where pictures let Rihannaholics post snaps of themselves with their idol from 'meet and greet' events.

*'It's f*****g Twitter, not the altar! Calm down.'*

[Later] 'Babygirl I'm sorry, I didn't mean to hurt or offend u! Just needed to make it clear to the [fans] … xoxo' Rihanna

Further Collaborations

In February 2010 Rihanna won another Grammy Award for 'Run This Town', her collaboration with Jay-Z and Kanye West. She then spent much of the year recording both the follow-up album to *Rated R* and appearing on a succession of collaborative singles and tracks. First off was the charity single to aid the victims of the Haitian earthquake, where Rihanna linked with Jay-Z and Bono and The Edge from U2 on 'Stranded (Haiti Mon Amour)', which became a minor UK hit in February, spending a single week at No. 41. Far greater success was achieved by teaming up with a revitalized Eminem on 'Love The Way You Lie'. The musical marriage between Eminem and Rihanna worked to perfection, giving Eminem his biggest selling single since 'The Real Slim Shady' and allowing Rihanna to put the temporary blip that was *Rated R* behind her. 'Love The Way You Lie' was a US chart topper and reached No. 2 in the UK. It would, however, spend some 43 weeks on the chart, as proof of its longevity.

Back On Form

If *Rated R* had been a dark album, largely written and recorded in the aftermath of her troubles with Chris Brown, then as far as Rihanna was concerned it was time to go back and have some fun. That was the game plan she laid down to the various writers and producers who would be responsible for crafting *Loud*; it was time to enjoy recording again.

Rihanna also took a much more hands-on approach to the album, serving as executive producer and therefore being almost entirely responsible for the way the album sounded, looked and performed. More importantly, this had to be a successful album, one to prove to her fanbase that she could still be relied upon to come up with the goods; every track had to stand out as a potential single, with no filler material.

A Thrilling Recording

Unlike previous albums, *Loud* was recorded in a wide variety of studios, as Rihanna had to fit in recording sessions around her Last Girl On Earth Tour. The sessions began in February 2010 and, with the album scheduled for a November release, had to be wrapped up by August at the very latest, which made for an extremely hectic recording schedule. There was to be a greater coherency to this album than any previous ones, even though around 200 songs were written for it before the best 11 were picked. Def Jam would later claim that they had used Michael Jackson's *Thriller* as a template – the album was laden with potential singles.

A Single Girl

The lead single chosen was 'Only Girl (In The World)', written by Crystal Johnson, Stargate and Sandy Vee; Rihanna felt so confident about this song that she selected it as a potential single before it had even been recorded. Inspired in part

'I think a lot of people have a *misperception* of me. They only see the *tough*, *defensive*, *aggressive* side. But every woman is *vulnerable*. So of course I'm going to have *that* side.'

Rihanna

because of the lack of uptempo material on the previous album, it was the first completed song for the new album and chosen as the lead single almost immediately. 'Only Girl In The World' did not shake the confidence placed in it, topping the charts in both the UK (for two weeks) and the US (for a single week, although this was achieved after the success of the second single, 'What's My Name?'). It would go on to attain platinum status in both territories, making it one of Rihanna's most successful singles of all time and proof that she was back to her winning ways.

'I called my new album Loud because it was a really fun, expressive album, and loud was the perfect word to symbolize that. We had fun the whole time. And you hear it when you listen to the songs.'

Rihanna

'I'm just gonna be *me*, because that's what *you guys* love the most, and that's what makes *me feel best*. Just being *normal*; normal for me is *Loud!* *Sassy, fun, flirty, energetic.*' Rihanna

Loud And Louder

With 'Only Girl In The World' vaulting up the singles charts, attention turned to the newly released album – would it be a triumphant return? Anticipation reached fever pitch in the US, with sales of 207,000 units in the first week that surpassed Rihanna's previous best and sent the album into the *Billboard* Top 200 at No. 3, which would be its peak. Once again, Europe in particular took to the new and revitalized Rihanna and *Loud*, which entered the UK chart at No. 2 behind Take That's *Progress*. Despite having only five weeks of sales between release and the end of the year, the album shifted sufficient copies to become the fourth bestselling album of the year. Two weeks later it traded places with Take That, becoming the second Rihanna album to top the UK chart and spending three weeks at the summit. While the album has so far sold 1.4 million copies in the US, in the UK it has surpassed this, shifting an astonishing 1.5 million copies – not far short of sales achieved by *Good Girl Gone Bad*.

All-format Domination

As had been the case with previous Rihanna releases, each successive single served to propel album sales ever upwards. 'What's My Name?', with Drake, was the second single lifted from the album and was immediately accepted at radio, so much so that it overtook the still-rising 'Only Girl In The World' and landed at No. 1 in the US before the lead

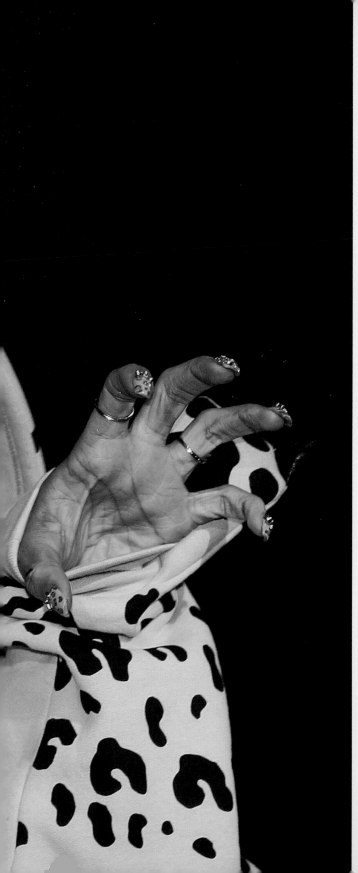

single – the first time in US chart history that such a thing had occurred. Its progress in the UK was rather more sedate, entering the chart at No. 18 on 27 November, hitting No. 2 behind television talent-contest winner Matt Cardle on the last chart of the year and finally ascending to the top spot three weeks into the New Year. This gave Rihanna both the No. 1 single and album in the same week and, with 'Only Girl In The World' also a resident in the Top 10 at the same time, a notable degree of dominance of the UK chart.

'I'm done recording the whole album. I made sure not to let you down with my music! You guys are always defending me, so now you've got some great songs to justify it.' Rihanna

Censored For Airplay

Domination was much the subject of the next single lifted from the album: the overtly sexual 'S&M'. Despite the nature of the track, the overall feel was sufficient to send it up to No. 3 in the UK and earn a silver disc. In the US the track did even better, powering its way to No. 1 and enabling

Rihanna to become the youngest artist ever to have achieved 10 US chart toppers, ahead of Mariah Carey. As the video was deemed 'inappropriate for some users' by YouTube, they insisted viewers must verify being 18 or older before watching it. The singer herself responded to the reaction and YouTube's decision by using her favoured means of communication, as usual: Twitter. 'U can now view the "S&M" video on Rihannanow.com UNFLAGGED!!!' She also tweeted, 'They watched "Umbrella" … I was full nude.'

Back On Top

February 2011 found Rihanna again very much in the spotlight as the awards season reached its zenith, with no fewer than four nominations at the Grammy Awards and due to appear performing twice: with Drake on 'What's My Name?' and with Eminem on 'Love The Way You Lie'. This latter track had received no fewer than five nominations in various categories, including Best Video and the prestigious Record of the Year and Song of the Year. Unfortunately, it was defeated in all five, although neither Eminem nor Rihanna would end the evening empty-handed. Her other nomination came for 'Only Girl (In The World)' in the Best Dance Recording category. Rihanna was on hand to collect the award – the fourth Grammy of her career.

'I didn't want to go backward and remake Good Girl Gone Bad. I wanted the next step in the evolution of Rihanna, and it's perfect for us. Get Loud everybody, get crazy, get excited, because I'm pumped!'

Rihanna

UK Recognition

Rihanna had been invited to perform at the 2011 BRIT Awards ceremony on 15 February. For the show, Rihanna decided to perform a medley of the three massive singles from the *Loud* album: 'Only Girl (In The World)', 'S&M' and 'What's My Name?'. She had originally intended to perform 'S&M' on its own but, after complaints about her outfit on *The X Factor* the previous December and the suggestive dance routine, she decided to tone down both the material and her look. The performance was still well received and the icing on the cake that evening was the award for Best International Female – the first BRIT Award Rihanna had ever won. It was perhaps the most apt award of her career, for she had been undoubtedly the leading international female of the previous few months.

Collaborations And Singles

Before the Grammy and BRIT Awards ceremonies, Rihanna had appeared on another major hit single, guesting with French DJ and producer David Guetta on his hit 'Who's That Chick?', which became a UK No. 6 in January 2011. A more modest hit was achieved with Kanye West on his 'All Of The Lights' track, which reached No. 15 in the UK in April 2011. As if to prove that *Loud* could still churn out hit singles, three further tracks have appeared in the UK charts during the course of 2011. The best performing was 'California King Bed', which returned Rihanna to

'I wanted a mixture of mid-tempo and uptempo stuff. I wanted a colorful album. I wanted every song to have its own subject, its own story, its own look, its own sound ...' Rihanna

the Top 10 and hit No. 8, well ahead of its peak in the US, where it stalled at No. 37. The UK has also seen chart appearances for 'Man Down' and 'Cheers (Drink To That)'. The overall effect of the singles lifted from *Loud* has been to return Rihanna to the very forefront of the charts all across the world.

A Field Of Her Own

Rihanna was filming a video for 'We Found Love' in September 2011 in a field in Northern Ireland when the owner of the field, farmer Alan Graham, turned up and ordered her to cover up. Hundreds of fans and onlookers had arrived at the farm near Bangor in County Down to have a look. The farmer, who had given permission for the video shoot, felt Ri running round in her underwear was 'inappropriate'.

When 'We Found Love' hit No. 1 in October 2011, Rihanna became the first female solo artist to top the UK chart six times in five consecutive years, having scored with 'Umbrella', 'Take A Bow', 'Run This Town', 'Only Girl (In The World)' and 'What's My Name?' between 2007 and 2011. 'We Found Love', the lead track from *Talk That Talk* (her sixth studio album, released in November 2011), sold over 87,000 copies in just four days.

Big Screen Battleships

Having made something of a cameo appearance in *Bring It On: All Or Nothing*, films seemed an obvious area for

Rihanna to pursue at some point in her career and it was subsequently announced that she had landed a starring role in *Battleship*, a film scheduled for release in 2012. Based on the game of the same name, Rihanna plays the role of GM2 Raikes alongside Liam Neeson, Taylor Kitsch and Alexander Skarsgård in the film by Peter Berg that has reportedly been given a $200 million production budget. Filming was slotted into a heaving schedule, alongside touring and planning *Talk That Talk*. The last few years have been exciting and successful ones for Rihanna; fans can expect – and demand – more of the same.

'Success for me isn't a destination it's a journey. Everybody's working to get to the top but where is the top? It's all about working harder and getting better and moving up and up.'

Rihanna

Further Information

Rihanna Vital Info

Birth Name Robyn Rihanna Fenty
Birth Date 20 February 1988
Birth Place Saint Michael, Barbados
Nationality Barbadian
Height 1.73 m (5 ft 8 in)
Hair Colour Brown
Eye Colour Hazel

Discography

Albums & EPs

Music of the Sun (2005)

A Girl Like Me (2006)

Good Girl Gone Bad (2007)

Good Girl Gone Bad: The Remixes (2009)

Rated R (2009)

Rated R: Remixed (2010)

Loud (2010)

No. 1 Singles

2005: 'Pon de Replay' (No. 1)
2006: 'SOS'
'Unfaithful'
2007: 'Umbrella (featuring Jay-Z)
'Don't Stop The Music'
2008: 'Take A Bow'
'Disturbia'
'Live Your Life' (T.I. featuring Rihanna)
2009: 'Run This Town' (Jay-Z featuring Rihanna & Kanye West)
'Russian Roulette'
2010: 'Rude Boy'
'Love The Way You Lie' (Eminem featuring Rihanna)
'Only Girl (In The World)'
'What's My Name?' (featuring Drake)
2011: 'S&M'
'Man Down'

Awards

American Music Awards

2007: Favorite Soul/R&B Female Artist
2008: Favorite Pop/Rock Female Artist
Favorite Soul/R&B Female Artist
2010: Favorite Soul/R&B Female Artist

BET Awards

2009: Viewers' Choice Award 'Live Your Life'
2010: Viewer's Choice Award 'Hard'
Best Female R&B Artist

BET Hip-Hop Awards

2009: Best Hip-Hop Collaboration 'Live Your Life'
Best Hip-Hop Video 'Live Your Life'

Billboard Music Awards

2006: Female Artist of the Year
Pop 100 Artist of the Year
Female Hot 100 Artist of the Year
Hot Dance Airplay Song of the Year 'SOS'

2007*: Hot Dance Airplay Song of the Year 'Umbrella'

2008*: Female Artist of the Year

Pop 100 Artist of the Year

Female Hot 100 Artist of the Year

Top Digital Song Artist of the Year

2009: Top Digital Song Artist of the Decade

2010: Top Dance Club Artist

Top Female Artist

2011: Top Rap Song 'What's My Name'

(*selected)

BRIT Awards

2011: Best International Female Artist

Grammy Awards

2008: Best Rap/Sung Collaboration 'Umbrella'

2010: Best Rap/Sung Collaboration 'Run This Town'

2011: Best Dance Record 'Only Girl (In The World)'

MOBO Awards

2006: Best R&B Artist

2007: Best International Act

MTV Europe Music Awards

2006: Best R&B Artist

2007: Ultimate Urban

MTV Video Music Awards

2007: Monster Single of the Year 'Umbrella'

Video of the Year 'Umbrella'

MuchMusic Video Awards

2006: Best International Artist Video 'SOS'

2008: Best International Artist Video 'Don't Stop The Music'

Most Watched Video 'Umbrella'

People's Choice Awards

2008: Favorite R&B Song 'Shut Up And Drive'

2010: Favorite Music Collaboration 'Run This Town'

2011: Favorite Pop Artist

Favorite Music Video 'Love The Way You Lie'

Favorite Song 'Love The Way You Lie'

Soul and Jazz Awards

2010: Best R&B Album of the Year *Loud*

Best Soul/R&B Artist of the Year

Best Collaboration 'What's My Name'

Teen Choice Awards

2006: Female Breakout Artist

Choice R&B Artist

2007: Choice R&B Artist

Choice Summer Song 'Shut Up And Drive'

2010: Choice Music: Rap/Hip-Hop Track

'Love The Way You Lie'

World Music Awards

2006: World's Best Selling Barbadian Artist

2007: Entertainer of the Year

World's Best Selling Pop Female Artist

World's Best Selling R&B Female Artist

Urban Music Awards

2007: Best R&B Act

2009: Best Music Video 'Rehab'

Best Female Act

Tours

Rihanna: Live in Concert Tour: July–September 2006; North America

Good Girl Gone Bad Tour: September 2007–January 2009; Worldwide

Last Girl on Earth Tour: April 2010–March 2011; Worldwide

Loud Tour: June–December 2011; Worldwide

Online

rihannanow.com:

Rihanna's official site, there is everything you need to know about this island girl turned international superstar

rihannadaily.com:

Unofficial site packed with news and information, including a tour-date calendar

ultimate-rihanna.com:

All the latest photos and gossip, with links to her Twitter and Facebook sites

@rihanna:

Join 8 million others and follow all Rihanna's Twittering

facebook.com/rihanna:

Get exclusives, sneak previews and up-to-date postings

myspace.com/rihanna:

Listen to your favourite Rihanna songs, for free!

Biographies

Michael Heatley (Author)

Michael Heatley edited the acclaimed *History of Rock* partwork. He is the author of over 100 music biographies, as well as books on sport and TV. His acclaimed biography of late DJ John Peel sold over 100,000 copies, while *Michael Jackson – Life Of A Legend 1958–2009* topped the *Sunday Times* bestseller lists and has been widely translated.

Graham Betts (Co-Author)

Graham Betts entered the music industry as a press officer with Pye Records. He went on to work for CBS Records (where he was Head of Press) and a number of other labels. He has written for numerous magazines and publications, including *Blues & Soul, Record Buyer* and *The History Of Rock*. He has also had more than 20 books published under his own name.

Mango Saul (Foreword)

Mango Saul has been a music, lifestyle and entertainment journalist for ten years. Some of his highlights include having breakfast at Waffle House with rapper Ludacris in Atlanta, sharing a bed with Destiny's Child for a *Smash Hits* cover interview and being sent an ice-cream costume for no reason. As Editor of Sugarscape.com, Mango has seen the site grow to over 4 million page views per month and was shortlisted for Digital Editorial Individual 2011 at the AOP Awards.

Picture Credits